What was it like...

In the street

Heinemann
LIBRARY

Louise and Richard Spilsbury

H www.heinemann.co.uk/library
Visit our website to find out more information about Heinemann Library books.

To order:
☎ Phone 44 (0) 1865 888066
🗎 Send a fax to 44 (0) 1865 314091
💻 Visit the Heinemann Bookshop at www.heinemann.co.uk/library to browse our catalogue and order online.

First published in Great Britain by Heinemann Library, Halley Court, Jordan Hill, Oxford OX2 8EJ, a division of Reed Educational and Professional Publishing Ltd. Heinemann is a registered trademark of Reed Educational & Professional Publishing Ltd.

OXFORD MELBOURNE AUCKLAND JOHANNESBURG BLANTYRE
GABORONE IBADAN PORTSMOUTH (NH) USA CHICAGO

Designed by Celia Floyd
Originated by Ambassador Litho Ltd
Printed in Hong Kong/China

ISBN 0 431 14823 6 (hardback) ISBN 0 431 14833 3 (paperback)
07 06 05 04 03 07 06 05 04 03
10 9 8 7 6 5 4 3 2 10 9 8 7 6 5 4 3 2 1

British Library Cataloguing in Publication Data
Spilsbury, Louise
   Streets. – (What was it like in the past?)
   1. Streets – History – Juvenile literature
   I. Title II. Spilsbury, Richard
   388.4'11'09

Acknowledgements
The Publishers would like to thank the following for permission to reproduce photographs:
Collections: Lawrence Englesberg 26; Corbis: Adam Woolfitt 29; Corbis: Bettman Archive 7 ; Hulton Archive: 6, 8, 9, 12, 13, 14, 15, 18, 19, 20, 23; Impact: Alex Macnaughton 25; Oxford Picture Library: 4, 5; Photofusion: David Montford 24; Stone: 28; The Francis Frith Collection: 10, 11; Topham: 16, 17, 21, 22, 27

Our thanks to Stuart Copeman for his help in the preparation of this book.

Cover photograph reproduced with permission of Topham.

Contents

Words printed in **bold letters like these** are explained in the Glossary.

Each **decade** is highlighted on a timeline at the bottom of the page.

Then and now

How do you think streets today are different from streets in the past? Streets have changed over the last 100 years because the way people live has changed. One of the biggest changes to streets is the kind of **transport** people use.

*This is the Royal Exchange, London at the beginning of the **century**. There are lots of horses and carts but no cars.*

1900   1910   1920   1930   1940

This is how the Royal Exchange in London looks now. There are lots of buses and cars but not a horse in sight!

In 1900 most people used horses and carts or walked on the streets. By 2000 streets were full of cars, buses, motorbikes, vans and lorries. In this book we will be thinking about lots of other ways in which streets were different in the past.

1900s: City streets

In 1900, horses pulled most of the traffic on city streets. Horses pulled delivery carts and buses for carrying people. Some people were paid to sweep horse droppings off the streets. Many streets were made from **cobbles**. When the wheels and horses' hooves rattled over the stones it was very noisy.

*In some streets there were **stables** for the horses and places for them to drink.*

Before 1900 most streets were unlit at night. By the 1900s some streets had electric lights, but most were lit with **gas lamps**. A lamplighter walked along lighting the lamps every evening.

One child remembers following the lamplighter home:
'I had to walk 2 and a half miles home from school, usually with a friend. What we enjoyed was following the lamplighter on his round. He carried a long pole with a shielded light at the top which he poked into the lamp and lit the gas **mantle**.'

1900s: Rich and poor

In the 1900s, many poor people lived in small **terraced** houses on narrow streets. None of these houses had electricity and few had taps indoors.

'When I was eight I used to carry six buckets of water every morning and evening from the conduit (tank) for which they paid me sixpence a week.'

Mr Sydney Bell, born in 1903

Terraced houses are joined together in rows, like these houses.

Carts carrying coal were a common sight on city streets.

Richer families lived in wider streets in much bigger houses. A few of these homes had electric lights and even telephones. Most houses still used coal for heating and cooking. Coalmen delivered coal by horse and cart.

1910s: Village streets

Village streets are not as busy as streets in towns and cities. In many villages in the 1910s there was no **public transport**. To get anywhere most people had to walk. Postmen delivered letters by bicycle and many doctors visited their patients on horseback.

In the 1910s, village streets were very quiet. People walked and played in the roads.

1900   **1910**   1920   1930   1940

People could often find everything they needed in their local village.

Villages in the 1910s provided everything for the people who lived there and on farms nearby. Almost every village had its own school, inn, shop and church.

In the 1910s, almost everyone went to church. When the bell rang for church on a Sunday morning, the villagers all walked to church wearing their best clothes.

1920s: Out and about

In the 1920s, more people went into town and city centres to shop. There were **markets** selling fresh food from around the country. There were lots of small shops that sold only one sort of thing, such as newspapers or cloth. Big **department stores** opened that sold lots of different things all under one roof.

Look at the kinds of vehicles that were on city streets in the 1920s.

In the 1920s some cities had as many as 30 cinemas!

There were not many restaurants in the 1920s. People did not eat out very often, but almost everyone went to the cinema at least once a week. Most towns and cities had several cinemas. A ticket cost just a few pence and films were in black and white with no sound.

1930s: New homes

By the 1930s there was better **public transport**. People could get to work more easily so did not have to live in city centres. Lots of streets were built on the edge of cities in the 1930s, nearer to the countryside. These housing areas were called **suburbs**.

This new street of houses was built in the 1930s.

More families owned their own cars. People parked their car on the street and some new houses even had garages.

Houses in suburbs had more space around them than the old **terraced** houses. Many had gardens at the front and back. Trees were also planted along the pavements.

People who had a car were very proud of it and kept it very clean!

1940s: Wartime streets

Between 1939 and 1945, Britain was at war with Germany. This was known as the Second World War. German planes dropped **bombs** on Britain.

At night people tried to make streets as dark as possible so the pilots flying the planes could not see where they were. This was called 'the blackout'.

Wardens had to make sure that people knew when to put up their blackout curtains.

Whole streets of houses were destroyed by bombs.

To keep the streets completely dark at night, the streetlights were not turned on. Trees and streetlights were painted with white rings to help **pedestrians** see them more easily. Vehicles out at night had to have special covers over the top of their headlamps.

1950s: Having fun

In the 1950s, few families had their own televisions and children did not have many toys. After school and at weekends most children played games, like skipping, in the street with their friends.

In the 1950s many streets were still quiet enough for children to play safely in.

In the past people often held street parties to celebrate important events. In 1953, Elizabeth II was crowned Queen of England. Parties were held in streets all over the country. The **Union Jack** flag hung from many buildings and everywhere was decorated with its colours – red, white and blue.

Everyone came to their street party in 1953.

1950 | 1960

1960s: Changes

By the 1960s, many streets had changed. Tower blocks were being built. These were high buildings with lots of flats where people lived.

By the 1960s most homes had black and white television sets, so TV aerials appeared on roofs. More people had telephones than before, so every street had telephone poles and wires.

Most of the tower blocks we see in streets today were built in the 1960s.

This supermarket is in a shopping precinct.

Some towns and cities had special shopping streets where no cars were allowed, only **pedestrians**. These were called shopping precincts.

At one time, people shopped for food every day. Now more people had fridges and freezers to keep food fresh. They went to the new big supermarkets to buy enough food for a week.

1970s: Traffic

By the 1970s there was a lot of traffic on the streets. People had to find ways of making the streets safer. They built more zebra crossings. The black and white zebra stripes and flashing lights warned drivers to stop if people wanted to cross the road. How do people help you to be safe on the streets today?

A lollipop lady helping children cross the road safely.

Lines on the street tell people where to park.
Two yellow lines mean 'No parking here'.

Traffic wardens are people who make sure drivers do not park their cars in the wrong place. This is important. If someone parks their car in a bad place, it could stop a fire engine getting to a house on fire at the end of a narrow street.

1980s: Living on the streets

By the 1980s, thousands of people were living on the street. People became **homeless** for different reasons. Some people lost their jobs and could not pay for their house anymore. Some people found that there was not room for them in the family home when they grew up. Sometimes they did not get on with their parents and did not want to stay.

Many young people lived on the streets in the 1980s and many do today as well.

1900   1910   1920   1930   1940

Vans deliver food and blankets to help some of the homeless people who live on city streets.

Living on the streets is hard. People get cold and uncomfortable sleeping outside. Without a job, you don't earn money to buy food or warm clothes.

Some **charities** help people who live on the streets. Helpers give out clothes and blankets, hot food and drinks or help people find a place to live.

1990s: Big cities

Millions of people live in big cities like Edinburgh, London and Cardiff. Streets are so busy, that many people find it easier to travel around on **public transport** like buses or underground trains. Some cities have **trams**. Trams had been used in the first part of the **century** but were then stopped.

A tram is a kind of bus that moves along tracks in a street.

Some restaurants look the same in every city.

Big city shopping streets in the 1990s were very different from the 1900s. New shops opened selling computers and mobile phones. Many new restaurants or cafes were parts of international chainstores. This means that a restaurant in one city looks the same and serves exactly the same food as one in another city. Do you shop in any chainstores?

2000s: Streets today

In the 100 years between 1900 and 2000 streets changed in many ways. In 1900 there were very few cars. Not all streets were lit at night. Those that were had **gas lamps**, not electricity as they do today. In 1900, horses were a common sight. Today, you are less likely to see a horse in a town or city.

Today, streets and houses are brightly lit by electric lights.

In some streets the buildings have changed very little. Next time you are in a street, take a look around. Which buildings do you think have been there a long time? Which are newer?

There may also be some buildings in a street that are the same outside as they were in the past, but which are used differently today. For example, some old cinemas are now bingo halls.

*These **terraced** houses were built in the early part of the century. They have heating and bathrooms now, but from the outside they look the same!*

Find out for yourself

There are lots of ways you can find out about the past. You could ask your parents or grandparents what they remember about streets when they were young.

Ask people you know if they have any photographs of their homes or streets. Older photographs will be in black and white, but they can tell you a lot about what kinds of vehicles were in streets in the past and how people got around.

Books

History from Photographs: In the High Street, Hodder Wayland, 1999

In Grandma's Day: Shopping, Evans, 1997

Fifty Years Ago: In the High Street, Hodder Wayland, 1998

Yesterday and Today: Going Shopping, Franklin Watts, 1998

Glossary

bombs when bombs hit the ground they explode and destroy everything nearby

century one hundred years. The 20th century means the 100 years between 1900 and 2000.

charities groups of people who work together to help others

cobbles round stones that were laid close together in rows to make a road

decade ten years. The decade of the 1910s means the ten years between 1910 and 1920.

department store big shop with lots of small areas inside, each selling one type of thing, for example, shoes or toys

gas lamps lamps that make light by burning gas

homeless when someone has nowhere to live

mantle a net tube that glows when you light it

market places where people sell food and other things from stalls instead of shops

pedestrians people who are walking in a street

public transport bus or train. You usually have to buy a ticket to travel on public transport.

stables places where horses can rest

suburbs streets on the edge of the city

terraced houses built joined together in rows

trams kind of bus that runs on electricity and moves on tracks along a street

transport vehicles, such as cars, buses or bikes

Union Jack the British flag

Index